NOTA

Martin Corless-Smith

FENCEbooks

Cover photograph by	Martin Corless-Smith
Author photograph by	Garrett O'Dell
Published in the United States by	Fence Books 14 Fifth Avenue, #1A New York, NY 10011 www.fencebooks.com
Book design by	Rebecca Wolff
Fence Books are distributed by	University Press of New England www.upne.com
Fence Books are printed in Canada by	Westcan Printing Group www.westcanpg.com

Library of Congress Cataloguing in Publication Data
Martin Corless-Smith [1965–]
Nota / Martin Corless-Smith

Library of Congress Control Number: 2002111805

ISBN 0-9713189-7-2

First Edition

Your enjoyment of the world is never right, till every morning you awake in Heaven; see yourself in your Father's Palace; and look upon the skies, the earth, and the air, as Celestial Joys: having such a reverend esteem of all, as if you were among the Angels.

—Thomas Traherne, *Centuries III*

one is trying to make a shape out of the very things of which one is oneself made.

—David Jones, *The Anathemata*

About the cover of this book there went
out off my eyes ill focus'd past
a drab shadow or stretchéd creature now
sent away without my [holding] fast

A fly disturb this room
a tear in the material
of all this room
a blur through which I am

Do I remember clear
enough we had each other
[and] then sitting at my chair
You not here

❖

I was looking back
to half a century
before me
why
This all before me

somebody's reason comes floating close

"BUT ALTHOUGH THE EXPERIENCE OF SEEING IS NOT TYPICAL"

Two feet above the ground I walk
invisible
a storm comes on in yellow light
thick drops

If I must sleep in daylight
and silent through my talk
the books I open follow
me as clouds

"ANY SEGREGATED WHOLE"

a light shining on them from behind
That they do not themselves (of) glow
held up in radiance of kind
dull metal will the lightest show

When you have read "A Life"
myself distracted by the sink
when you recall the moment someone said
or then decide there is a way to move

❖

I haven't been ~~alive for ten years now~~
The habit ~~that required me~~ was required by me
~~And habits whether red or green accept so little light~~
with which to make this sandy only shallow growth
(which will allow this sandy shallow plot to grow)

There are also solitary bees
those whose soil is so poor
ant on the cut peony
carried off in folds of
scent from the earth

In rare cases it is useful to talk

---

there is an S at the side of the Word
The shop sign
So S Slips sturdy / glistening
off to the world
My foil fell sideways
revealing a web acxross the face
hasten now hair follicles
erect a forest in the space
an archipelago

"Give place to me that I may dwell"

The symbolic landscape of the landless
The principal possessions of the dispossessed

The Subject propos'd
And even rising with the rising mind
With inward view circled with Inflected View
A Prospect of the fading Woods. Enlivened Woods

We are all grown into the world
of given green
our dearest colours not our own
we know ourselves as others know

❖

The invisible wedge comes into us
my one eye over there
By cover of costume, customs and variety of pose
the arrows met Sebastian and make it so

NOTA

The authority I give to OR is always as a subset of AND.

Any description of that which is becoming is thought inferior to a description of that which is.

Truth ~~is a fiction of expression.~~ It is the myth of the eternal in the World.

What the lyric says is not simply that I am going to die—but that to whomever reads this I am dead.

Otium cum dignitate

Matter ~~though independently real~~ is ~~dependent for meaning on its relation to~~ Spirit.

We are sisters——a lovely traveller at night
who might a taste of dying rape
a peep a piece of light hole
Champion all lame

Romanticism is the companion of Materialism.

If you will be your own Heaven you must last forever.

I have been flapping for a century. Inordinately. Flapping a small flag as to hold life up from the soil of death. but no matter. This tattered flag.

My teeth biting the spoon as hard as they can.

We use our families as an excuse. We use ourselves as an excuse.

What I like about birds is nothing. of which I am intent.

If you have not suffered from behind the indignities of the fuck
thrust from behind, the full throat
If you have never another inside
or the walk from that or walk to that

❖

a clamourous recognition threatens mè
to pain and hurt another as myself
fall I into or almost this
adrenalin

A TRAVELLER I AM
AND ALL MY TALE IS OF MYSELF

—William Wordsworth, *The Prelude 1805,* Book III

What was the first I never
knew the names of it
the matter was I never
want to read the fact
I was involved in preparation
am involved a moment knows
aged four a naked thunder storm
for hours though I do not count
aged four a golden bicycle
a blue hand-painted bicycle
a purple bicycle aged four
a train, a fort, a car
for any of these dearly dearly
Persons showing interest in
to me it was a pleasure
to be seen not being seen

I (may) have obliterated terror from the scene
or sad or failure both as true
It is a pleasant tale no less
this fabrication put up job
when I assumed enough was far too much
A head laid down upon the carpet seen the curtains net
The smell of sweat in overall arrives
the grime of years at work
and coming back why leave
it makes a trembling—returns
what makes it to my day
Do I recall the terror of the spoken need
or reading disappointment in remarks

marked down in lines for me I do not
often this the page was my forbidden fear
my ignorance or worse my tears to understand
and worse my almost understanding anything
the imposition of a voice upon my ear
my head—the larger hands around
the things done well the things forgotten then

Numina in place of time
arrive out of company or ill of sorts
the local boys all clamouring in violence
the bough up out towards away from town

These magnificent in fields
these blades that push against and part
this hard ground like scalp in clay
or all of these and rain

but never night was mine
or any many other places
til it came to York
For signs of former barracks buried now

the glorious new woman on the face of it
the uniform desire of taking part

If you will drop me down slow to the low chair
the cinema undoes your done up front
and proves a public venue for your cunt and pubic
beneficiary you beautiful and new as me

So love become an inventory of those
Surrounding me a duty to preserve
to purchase stores of this perfection
for some other life

I become the painter of a scene
thankyou for accepting me
thus a status is conferred inferred
and this is borrowed for my means

A young man tries on sex
the boy was still infront of trees
Religion that he made for this
one or two companions he had met

Reading could have been another town
The dictionary dome or capital
which neither welcomed me or let me go
And then America invaded home

But Have I missed it
lying down playing with care
drawing—having
this—Do it again

I must make this into something new
now in my middle years
and counting backwards counting is endured
Those that I walked with have expanded their estates
and we visit seldom put off at the gates

Those that occupy myself have dwindled
still—my ambition to be loved replaced
by the desire to be now left alone
all say a few but what I find
is that I cannot be that much even to so few

I might not have the chance

my head and body in each cell

this morning set out for the hill
this afternoon can only make it home

now settled on a bottle theme in brown
an English village or a seaside town

Is it what you thought
what you wanted when
you thought of what you
wanted now you ought to ask

A boy with a school tie is dressed forever thus
A boy adored will always want as much
noone has died although you know they must
Your confidence does not extend to trust

Then come down over me upon me now
a thought that might allow myself
no thought a passage where the walls without
a field where nothing borders nought

my soul a shoe a mouse
inside a shoe my obsessed body
ready for the ordinary
my mind obsessed with body ready

hung by a filament of thought
over yours and my own nakedness
walking out upon this ground
of us enacting our own grace or sacrifice

Dead in a moment Dead for the moment
risen like its twin inside itself
harboured in dry dock
rock and slick the firmament

Earth pour a solid liquid over me
a dustbowl drink out of
whenever held suspended over ocean
where aside of vanity

Over Windsor & Westminster
Abbey monstrous nobility
to land in London's window
as obsequious and Grand

the sky an earth the earth a sky
welcomes a returning Sun
the sliver Thames below
magestic sprout of trees

Now city newspapered and
little that I own to meet them on
they walk occasionally near to me
shirted in poss-impossibility

Can I say this
now never existed (now that never was)
words never meant their objects
You and I came into this

---

mouldering
The longest purse wins parliament
necessitating on it
O I want so much to do my meant

first the voice starts on
the orchestra joy joins in
choir share cello horn
my god we have begun again

I was passing this hedgerow hides
some house out in the hills
where someone had made money lives
And what shall I to enter this wall

I never did, though I pass the houses
empty as I sit each day
A park before a dog a pigeons joy
the houses and the cars around about

So my desire to die
to rest under my perfect land
to sit before or after with your wife
we weep or roar into the ground

cleave solitude and raise the house

ill of the orchard
its many posturing

(our son would not attain perfection)

A Selection from the
Works of Th^os. Swan
(MS. 8911 Worcester
City Records Office)

Saw a beautiful sphinx this evening flying about the flower its wings made a
     humming noise like a top its body fur
(I have no scientific names) was covered with a down of black and white

—*Notebooks*

I take myself up
          over cliff trees
as swimming
          a bright bursting off

For once at once your fear's day duplicates
          its Seemless Possiverities
all mingled like a calmless wealth
          Oh I am stalked

vision of a place
          this always-onning
lumbrous
          transparent over rocks

I cannot and run
          lingring of this steep
I cannot and go
          my Wings trained to a near invisibility

i take myself on up
over clifftrees off
a swimming brimming cup
a bright bursting off

O am I from above

my vision is a place
its ever shifting face
a waterfall she is

i cannot run and stay
this sudden steep so hill
I cannot stay and go

—*Poems in Manuscript*

I

On my brother W[illiam] falling from his horse

Was not the horses [sic] start
what made it start was not
A shadow or a hare afoot
as sense of something sudden near the heart   an arrow to the heart

You fell on your right side
to break your arm and dignity   pride
a fellow helped you catch your ride   that fellow caught your ride
who you did not know or see   yhom did not notice next to thee

before you fell. And afterwards
a different beast your horse   another horse your horse
and afterwards yourself somehow   and changed yourself somewhere
the earth had entered through your breast   restructured where it was

This land of yours no longer yours   each atom now itself
but you its curious gift   And you this curious gift
each leaf a painted diadem   each leaf a painted leaf
an atom in a leaf   miraculous & hidden shift

[To a friend]

Set it from your mind my sturdy friend
before this day is over set it out
that you may not another day as this day end
in furious retreat from what is done ~~is out~~   ~~(from what has beene)~~

Nothing one days deed enough to end a life   (no thing enough to end this life in
no more then one days meal can feed   some small deed)
you must as grateful as a giant Sun
Which more then all you have begins again

fieldnotes

—*Notebooks*

Swallow

Down momentarily and banks
itself the only mimick in the pond
of its cavorts the fly act randomly
which I cant love as much as thee

from a calandar of dayes

—*Notebooks*

January 16th

Margaret in her vineyard laugh[s] out loud
I here [sic] as ~~I~~ passing as I ever much [must?]
this sweet ~~song~~ soul married now
and laughing to herself at three of clock

[March 19th or 20th ?]

I have noticed ants today
all about the diary
as busy as our own busyness ~~(and ours a busy day)~~
I could not work for looking at their ways

[Days]

—from a MS. Addit. fragment.

The day ~~as is~~ a hand we recognize as ours
The day ~~is neither~~ not singular nor plural   The day not singular or more
The day ~~as~~[?] a song we near ~~cannot quite~~ recall   That
a weapon that reaches to us as we reach   a weapon ^we reach to reach
as a sturdy petal gained ~~and~~ regained in strength   a sturdy flower regained in strength
Immortal as man not as man   immortal Man impossible as man

The day a vast tree with a wasp-like waist {An Oak or Pear}
The day a spirit in a shell (vase) {a ~~faerie~~ whisper in a ~~faerie~~ ear}
The day a bell rings once at least {which makes both sides}
The day moves water north and west and south and east {the tides}
the day encounters of itself more (most) bravely {as an ant}
like the animal that faces death ~~impartial and in fury~~ {tiny Giant}
                    in impartial fury

natures fecuditie

In her perfect silks she comes to thee {me}
The Rose The Lily and The haw
Are garments of her spring attire
Which she disrobes at summers door
~~The~~ to soak in her fecundity
Whereon the golden gown of her maturity she
takes   ~~before~~ the Wheat ~~as~~ field as her crown before
          The autumn ~~fades~~ [illeg. struck-through] begs her to retire
          disrobed once more upon the threshers ~~millers~~ floor
~~Where as she steps outside her gown She~~
~~is no more~~
                    ~~as we acquire~~
                              ~~our store~~
~~and thus eternally~~

~~She dies as we acquire our bread her seed~~

Where as she steps outside herself she
dies in faith of her own seed
which is our ~~need~~ bread

                          ✫

The boundaries of forgivenesse need not be confused with those of
knowledge

I am overrun with petynesses—a hovering image of my alternative grace
the most galling.

11,000 leaves of Chryst   11,000 words for leave
doe, sow, green, house, glass, post, post, highly heaven

7 million piece of bark   7 millions bits of piece of beech

thrush, caw, dun, haw, thorn, crush, toe, delve, harrow, hand

10,000 yrs of days   10 million days of hours

bayleaf, churchdoor, shade, caitiff, sign, whore, pool, leaf

A fool I am without concern   fond thoughtless fool without within   when

I become this tree

Helm dungeon mansion, realm, magnificat, height, moon, nurse, land

11,000 me in light   two skies of blue for sight
ocean of spit   lims up and down as roots
lined skin grown out   An Ocean on the land am I
Our ship upin the Skye   27,000 saints at sail
From 27,000 gales   This tree on which our Lord
Still dies   this ship   that fires for thee

11,000 whisperers   A hymn above the floor
3,000 whisperers   A hymn above the ceiling of the tree
1,000 whispers   The ship, The Tree Our ~~Song~~ Skye

Car fellow day swallow milk fallow dart hallow

Epistle of the Martyr [Possibly an erroneous title]

Flight is our true response unto a tree
We cannot help outside—Our Passions unify
In natural union all we see
Our understanding underneath one aspect of iternity

Bliss is our true response unto a Day
Trades shall adorn our spacious land
Tasks shall equip us with our true duty   tasks are our true identity
As our perfection in obscurity is grand

My soft ignorance is true response unto our Lord
Ask is a sparowe how the hawthorn ~~grew~~ grows   as is a sparowe
Take note that through I give the word
I only hand on as the sparrow ~~knew~~ knows

My soul stands at the side of this
A word my ear has heard and passed along
For in our day we cannot alter bliss
Nor hold onto the mirth that is a song

A True metaphor for our Lord

In side a Country In a lake upon an Island
Sits and stands an oak which was not planted there
For our alone in side that oak upon a branch and
By a leaf a bird which was not placeed there
Sings upon a note upon a sound for one listening
Who was not placed here but for all these happening

The Bee

From beds and borders bordering external waste
Our delving truth nods into everyness
Plain truth inticing as a spic'd perfume
To paint the desert a lush wilderness

Colours that do correspond not to the outward aspect though in truth I do see them so

PURPLE GOOSE (Purple is the most common colour to hover beneath a pure white essence)—thus is it with the lilly and the Sides of a new shorn Goat.

PINK OAK (Pink can be understood beneath the fur of a creature— Such as a rabbit or the chin feathers of a hen—but for my purpose I seek the hidden colour which is announced at the perypheries of sight). Of vision.

PINK beneath the wheat

PINK under earth (which makes it as I do suppose a giant creature laid out belly foremost to the sun—the hills such as a wrinkles in the spaniels neck)

GOLD EVERYTHING (which is the mastery of light—Evening light cannot be said only to reflect upon the surface of an arm as it might upon a night-pond—but it affect the subtle structure of a skin and comes not from upon but from within in equal parts also. See this upon a young ones arm or face—I dare say with a night-pond the day time store of light within is used up very immediately)

GOLD FLESH The human hide is more like cheese than milk—its solidity is a moment plucked out of fluid—fat chosen and suspended to our amazement. How more complicated this skimming of our solids into one animated whole. Integrity.—though not the surface of a metal—in this respect a pewter piece like an evening pond than like a face. Our elements are infected with light. Elemental to our surface animation is internal light.

Blue, pink and red grass—affected in the halo of a field by where it lays, its reach, drainage—the affect of soils—Some darker grasses are dark blue beneath and taste accordingly of night. Pink grasses are acid to the tongue.

BLUE EYES—this of birds and beasts—beneath there subtle stones a deep Blue lake (not the milk blue of an ancient hound) as though of yet not island to be found. Wings of the landing creatures are not ignorant of their relation to the currents in the air. The ether sensible to every creature upon its face.

Of various persons and their anterior colours

A person known to me of high regard—noticeable in the vicinty for his vocality is I have seen preceded and followed by a train of leaf green. This is the slightest of presences—invisible to the direct gaze—but it will happen as the air sucked after one who leaves a room.

The young likewise in general a light green to yellow.
Purple to dark for them quite ill or destitute. I have seen the colour in a dying face slip shadows from hues of energy to stale lifeless grey. I have no doubt that a spectrum of invisibility describes their inner state. And this spectrum awaits our perusal when we see fitly to concentrate our sights appropriately.

My hands some days glow full red as though at war with some internal flux. After a brisk walk the instrument of my vision may be most momentarily alert. I may go months across the surfaces of all objects alike—noticing only the regular structure of their impression.

Margaret is soft orange. William a fresh pale blue.

I am not incredulous to the ages of Methuselah Lamech Enos Mahalaleel or any of their tribe. Were one to concentrate 4thousand years might not seem sufficient for the fruitful examination of one tree. And one cannot die when concentrating thus. To be struck blind from behind, unknown in such a situation must surely result in the abandonement of some small part. It is fear I have felt the soul pushed to the very throat during terror for myself and those dear. This uppushing of the soul is it to say preserve that part which is the better. So I might pass out of myself just so into concentration merely—for in observing is it not so that I am my own body my eye as vehicle and that where I am taken to—a plum blossome who billows and dints in a breeze are felt equally by my vision as were a thorn to pass through my open palm. To my sight—which seems held in loose connection to my self the world is equally a home. My other senses, touch, taste, hearing, necessary is that other portion such is held or smelt or listened to. I AM NO FREE AGENCY. A sound announce itself upon me even as I listen for another—touch hazards sharp even as I think to swim exhilarating springs.

Neither all day can you recognize yourself. This arm in general aspect similar—but were I lent another of its shape would be me still?
This World & Body might seem all a borrowed shell of softest welcome though our dignity is of another order. Though I cannot hate such gifts.

A field of corn stub give up its smoke of blue as though these straws as chimneys to a further field. Stiff vein into a nether heart.

Then green laid lightly as linen on a violet place.

Once nature offered man a mirror for himself
or notice that his face is like her face
I take one make her in my own image
or shiver like the water as my foot goes in

the night exaggerates anxiety
a call to compromise
the richer universities
so beautiful and wise

Which one or both of us has died
The world and me
Suspended in inquiry while I
the gravity of a great roll

someone has fallen in the square
not that I saw or even knew
someone was passing underneath
and saw

and now of course the work to be less even than
the shyest soldier in an unreported war
the flood of history too early
for the tired

I am now quiet waiting for my visitor
it rains a little and I do not move
if only to make (notes for) this
(I will be) waiting for a while

How could his bearing now so damp
not weather—or the influence of others
but the draw and drain of want
love next to draughts under the cover (sea)

By way of cold I come I go
By way of coldness in this summerscape
Dear If I could any other be
I have no way. the changes are incorporate

yell provenance nee providence
An Island or a larger mass
We met mid conversation
as our memories were constitute

Five years ago (says Story) I lov'd you
will Story recognize us now or in five more
ten years ago (so Story says) I didn't know
nor thought to know today who makes me so

Both knowing (I think) at heart we will survive
if parted so you take that as base
and venture wreckless willingly on love
I take the base and use it as advise to move

Green spikes torture through the dirt
a warm deluge a loaf
the park and street
trembling lorry of a day without

some other coast or go
a meal is cheap
undo
with sleep

What I feel in the eye or face
The whole lot melts
ice falls
floor

down me please
my freezing deer
the tongue held out
stare

A Year has past
Tan and Red
fade
Chinese Theatre

There is a city I inhabit
concocted miraculous
a Pegasus. a Cerberus
where I am Thief and Saint

A Wholly living other walks my streets
acknowledges the local signs
ten hundred instants of the man he meets
his gestures given mine

will he touch for me myself
in conversation will he hold
his mind high in the thought
or

The real fish of my feet
who we forget to greet
are underneath me now
swimming the pavement

I would give up all
for me except myself
I am
I would give up

much less than other times
this felt to me the time
when I could touch to happiness
or pull a fluid from my breast

wretch—throw up the hound
the scuffle where I wade
made small small mouths
together end on end for months

If I do not It will catch
up If I do it is enough
The day still turns me over
out of enough

fiery burgesses comprise my audience
and so I look beyond this burden
to a sample of affectionate embrace
a quiet face to listen to

exaggerate my joy my possibilities
confound solutions with obscurities
a birth up hold a national guise
or job by which to know me by

a tenuous vehicle, a horse for war
the glory of the self is vanity
a glee which rises like a score
o only if a horse set out

Mixture of erudition and wildest speculation
piety, sympathy and charlatan
when his host and she at Ragley Hall descend
Her hair of dark and bosom open him

God on his knees devoured by rats
and fleas this woman spilled him from himself
unhook all else and wipe it clean she
in her recognition of his state

You ask you may you may survive this sight
you won't survive yourself and here you end
another takes you on you must comply
you have no other gravity

I find when I am done and spent eternity
my heart is youngest in its blood
My eats fucks shits what is beyond this state
what fits this body now is what I wear today

A genius describes a revolution
a raven flies
only as a farmer
plants to feed a regicide

---

futurity alone makes this bearable

there is an outrageousness at the centre of things, in history and the human mind, which only silence can accommodate

providence operates without visible regard for justice

"At the day of doom men shall be judged according to their fruits"

The man in rags
a scabbéd creep-hedge
"I once had land" but now
"I'm grown exceeding poor

nipples licked by a dog
mouth by a dog
arse and balls by a dog
desperate tongue takes over

magic nor knowledge fed the day
unhappy virtue flounders in its pen
The fox seizes morality
and rips its chicken throat open

I am tired over the city
and cannot climb
I am still tired in retreat
the victor and the vanquished are the same

fair enough
is it
are we a pair
of hero notes

labour not
nor animal
the trees themselves
and fruit abundantly

the self welcomed
to be eventual
it is depresses me
no, seriously

explanations come to
an end somewhere   Wittgenstein p3 Philosophical Investigations
a helpless meet a slack jacket
deboned chest filleted cheek

fear of
abandonment
of cowardice
my death

Where am I
[It is] not impossible that [truth] may have more shapes than one   J.M. Areopagitica
Have you Heard the curlew crazy overhead
noone in my family did anything

Are we as perfect as fruit
I cant stand myself by this machine
I see the contours of the hills in shire relief
Some blocks away a car horn and a dog

I keep expecting us to do and say the same thing which we do
My invented recollection of meeting you
some of your clothes are older than us
most of mine were made for someone else

plenum with eyes open
not through but over and around
Young Auden then his slippers came
Young Milton then his eyes switched off

The tongue is dead long live
the word for tongue
large rain drops on the pavement
warm we lick the sour spot

I think the idea of progress gives to the student or artist a feeling that his next picture must & will be much better than the last & this, I think, is not the right way to think of progress in art. I think an artist should seek first the kingdom of Heaven & then proceed to describe the many pleasing & varied things he sees there . . . first an awareness of the essential happiness in things, then a feeling of things being sacred & holy & then a feeling of being somehow cut off from these things. At this point my state would be very much like being in love . . . And I think an artist's life is very much a continual celebration of marriage between himself & what he wants to paint. All these feelings had a very quickening effect on my vision as they naturally would & I began to want to make things clear & definite.

—Stanley Spencer. *Numbered Writings*

UPON ACCUSATION

DEFEND: I do not see it so
                     Truth is particular, it visits one
                     in clothes another will not recognize
                     It was a jest

ACCUSE: Your gesture was too bold

DEFEND: In Truth no gesture is alone
                     Yet what it calls for anyone
                     as well as nobody can say

ACCUSE: Are you not architect of your own deed?

DEFEND: Aye, and builder—but the house
                     is empty till another fills it with her din

ACCUSE: You cannot shift so easy from your sin

DEFEND: I can sit or run, I say it thus
                     what I have done when said your way
                     I am the first to seize upon
                     but just as justice to another give
                     I will not hear my own trial overrun

ACCUSE: Then Speak

DEFEND: My story is as everyone's
                     though for that seldom heard
                     Some deeds run close to several aims
                     not one can singly be the cause
                     I have an instinct for complexity
                     It is not dishonesty. the plain tree
                     by light, by water, soil all is bourne up
                     I will not do in shade or sand

ACCUSE: You have said nothing

DEFEND:	Then I have said nothing wrong.
	I am undone for being so. I have some fear
	though doubt another hates me as I do
	this then be my sun. My land is common still
	and water is the tonic of another
ACCUSE:	Which you freely swim
DEFEND:	How free is it—were water censored
	would you die of thirst
ACCUSE:	Do you admit in metaphor your deed?
DEFEND:	Again we read each other's meaning for ourself
ACCUSE:	Then you cannot defend
DEFEND:	No, nor you condemn.

last night the very gods showed me
a face grown terrible & huge
look at me for consummation
a month I near don't recognize

I am unwound in girdles
my flesh swound in a giddy brew
I have become my other selfs enveloped self
and saddled as a scabbard to the hilt

what is my good name
what if it were none
beyond my help or claim
as general as a coloured stone

LETTER TO A.H.

My self—most often situated behind the eyes, in the head, when today, one eye in pain my self moves, slips onto the left rear shoulder perhaps. A sinister perch. The eye as enemy—Or my God where to pin it.

Monday March 19, 2000
My consciousness under a dim fog—as it flickers—the day not open to a self. As I sleep in the sun room a little glint in the dense blue flies, separated from the distant sound of its engine. On such gravity. And through a crack the world screens purple with a yellow hovering haze. The ports are deserted—a small boy is called in.

Here I write my future down. Which happens as I have predicted them.

By the summer of the year 2—he had finished his degree. His brain being used up—or his attention taken over with distractions and shadows, he was unable to focus for more than an hour or less at a time. He enjoyed particularly the tasks of a normal domestic nature—peeling potatoes—making tea—slicing cheese—or even a rigorous session of weeding, though he by no means enjoyed all tasks, nor those considered necessary—laundry he did not enjoy— and would hang clothes to air a number of times. He shaved two to three times a week—washed his hair less, and was forced, by vanity and their voracious growth to clip nails both toe and finger at least once a week. Something he had never given regular service to when younger. He imagined the toenails had grown peculiarly brittle and coarse through some neglect or dietary oversight. He was often surprised at their yellow curled vulgarity, remembering his nails pink and clear. His hair remained mostly thick—worrying him at times above the temples and on the very crown—though why he worried—vanity which is never afforded in accordance with any physical accuracy.

He had been in his own memory a happy person—but this had seemed insufficient at some stage in mid life and a habit of disappointment in others mixed with self loathing had resulted from an array of ordinary human interactions read as personal slights. In the end it did not go that well.

What of Hope?
In one version this becomes a euphemism for losing touch—in another it provides its own delights—an older man still active and attractive and engaged on projects for the sake of possibility alone.

What of Love?
Though gifted with something like a natural propensity to love and be loved it seemed never to announce itself fully. was hampered by frustrations, by details unresolved and unresolveable. Elsewhere he possessed to the end a delight in friendship, and an array of longstanding relationships which he visited throughout the years.

What of Children?
He had one, he had none. One died. Disappointed him. Preferred its mother—was angry—He realized at the instant of its birth it must die. Thought it would, knew it must. Never did.

Of the World?
It met him or he it at variance. He was protectively disillusioned— defensive in his ambitions—unhappy with his desires, with having and needing them. Refusing them he foundered in them—they matched his décor—of rented accommodation—middlingly pleasant—filled with an array of furniture which displayed necessity and accident rather than conspicuous design.

What of Death
Through neglect—through embrace—a culmination—a ruination—at a time of indifference—at a time of high stress—quietly at home in his garden. Forgotten.

The Next Category

or perhaps the first should be his companion—or companions—his wife or wives or loves. How the experiment flourished. Here was a resounding echo in the hall. I must love. I must. In youth in the uncertainties of a career or on a path—In the jealousies of desire and fear—in the cauldron of influence, the description and metadescription of a self alive. He must love—as only he and it can and will he—will it awaken him, in him, will it permit him, grant him. Them.

In vanity
buds unbuttoning
Around him are his
disappearing few

Can I wait here quiet in your company
a tick a pulse
tap leaks on the clock
a watch can tell us the minute

why even now I feel
I should a little further
and an idea will
explain this after all

a panic
hares heart
ripped across
your walk

In Solomon's Museum
de Umbris Idæarum
jellied air
our plenum

And thus my brother's crime I realize as mine
and wanting order was no substitute for love
and wanting to be right no closer than another's right
and waiting you to love you as myself

There are those, including often the self, who you cannot abide—but those, especially the self, that you must.

If you come any closer, come any closer, I cry out to myself, to anyone

This then with its open pleading—You cannot suffer away from this—you cannot.

A look from a not unattractive stranger which confers upon you that which you already possessed.

Consider the crippled Vargas
Philosopher of the elements
Venerable outdoorsman
arriving for the festival of lights

consider the dark night clowned in its robe
the beams and punctures hammering
left on the ledges of the house
down there below us as the tent takes shape

The young students dressed in archaic fashion
The symbol of a part accepted and one given
Great Vargas unknown noone qualifies to know
The festival itself a nominal show.

[I like it if it fall(s) down (a)round my waist]

Orpheus was son of Calliope the muse. Apollo it was presented him with a lyre—and the Muses taught him to use it. O Mother. O Son. Make of us what you will. With it he animated the inanimate.

The same poet hoped to fetch his wife Eurydice back from the dead such was his faith in his own powers of recollection. Hades imposed one condition. Not to look back. But a poet apostrophizing. To turn away from. Walking iambic, the line was forward but the rhyme reminded us. We read forward looking back.

The story ends with the cyclical nature of crops. Nostalgia. Verdant and verbose. Self-consciousness. Doubt in our future. Winter. Doubt that we can charm what we would most charm. Our mortality. The lyric out of time. Immortal. Doubt.

The Maenads tore him limb from limb. Set on him by Dionysius. Jealous of his singing. Drowns him in oblivion. The passionate devourers. His head floated free of his body singing. The poem sent from the body. His head was the oracle silenced by Dionysius. His lyre laid at the feet of Apollo.

Or Zeus killed him. Angered at secrets divulged. Singing his own elegy. A preacher. The trees danced in his music. How are we to read the dancing trees?—Here it is. The trees danced.

Envied by the gods. Born of them.

A child of four or less
reconstructed face
An anger brought down
on her victim-head

It is a poor connection I will try
back later when these pines
and undergrowth in sand
I will call you later on

Not a word of me
one more thing to say
or left un said
I am away from this

Players always were made undone
tricks make us kiss for joy one word
and images imagine us as one
another day is all we ever have

Was not the eagle or the cockatiel
it was the sparrow led me here

TO FOLLOW
SOME ELEMENTS THAT HAVE HITHERTO BEEN IGNORED
OR MISCLASSIFIED

GRASS: Of all abundance—most certainly an element. Long standing
and originator of the colour green. Element in rodent and mammal
life. Provider of nutrients (difficulty) and shelter. Can be broken
down into smaller particles but remains grass.

TREES: Abundant—misclassified most often through variance of
structure.

BIRDS: Abundant vociferous often agitated

WATER: Similar to above. Coterminous with Air

LIGHT: misclassified through microscopic rather than macroscopic
appreciation. particularly volatile. Extremely companionable with all
elements.

DRYNESS: Not to be mistaken for the presence of or abundance of
numerous smaller elements. Dryness is a common porousness in the
regular constitution. Results in evacuations and further
conglomerations. A state of illness.

ENERGY: name given to principle inhabitant

DREAM: Occurrence of residue similar to outer layer of abundance.

FOXING: magnification of odours

TALK: Efflorescence concomitant with ambition and / or Energy
for ambition see trajectory also amble.

HAIR: See further nails, skin, teeth and dissolution of grass.

ODOUR: Similar to talk.

—Johannes Vargas, notes for *Elementals*

There are two sorts of Eternity; from the Present backwards to Eternity and from the Present forwards, called by the Schoolmen Æternitas à parte ante, and Æternitas à parte post. These two make up the whole Circle of Eternity, which the present time cuts like a diameter, but poetry makes it extend to all Eternity to come, which is the half-Circle—A. Cowley.

as for our Reader. The reader makes that backwards trace.
Remis ego corporis utar
(I'll use the Bodies Oars)

London
have a stone
edifice
bronze gryphon

House has gone
The garden most intact
You haven't and you can
For ages gone inside

Shall nettles grow up on our Palaces
dock leaves in our factories
Mothers without accents in the streets
scholars still as babies

three places come to mind
a group of fish ponds covered by high summer shade (in Ombersley)
a former kitchen garden used as nursery for the parks (in Perdiswell)
A large Edwardian Riverside Estate part used as a retirement home
                                        (The end of Harbourne Terrace)

He lived in his hermitage, giving his entire attention, as he occasionally
told me, to thoughts which on the one hand grew vaguer day by day, and
on the other, grew more precise and unambiguous.

—W. G. Sebald *The Emigrants*

it is not exploration I desire—but routine in which to lose a self

A stable accumulation towards a coherency

grey morning in a city I will settle
Remnants of the industrial. A red brick
reputation slight in the environs nil abroad
a lightless grey taxi from the station

edwardian lined avenue
home to professors
though now numerous new
halls of residence and annexes

signs of former times
the massive rhododendrons
and the wash stand by
the kitchen door

the tannoy
voice
compartment to myself
air and spirit rush

---

coats dark room
strewn on bed of women's powder
entered slow by slow
an ache enact relief

What I'm drawn to again is a register of intent and presence

"It was the kind of thing that was moderately meaningful to a microscopically small percentage of the population at a particular moment."

"Someone witnesses something amazing, but what matters most is not 'out there' . . . but deep within, at the vital emotional centre of witness . . ."

"If one understands that when we speak of gardens we are asking 'how shall we feed ourselves.'"

"an ideal dependent upon the work of man and the corruptible contingency of Nature."

"The amorous thrills of the thrushes as though immanence were ceaselessly reworking and remodeling transcendence to the point of vertigo."

So that no one, because of the thick leaves could see me through them

All we can do is imitate sorrow

we will always wonder what made the horse shy in those empty fields

The qualities of emotion, then, varying as one bird song from another. Sorrow and elation separated by the slight tonal shift. A chord is struck and imagines itself. One bird song often constituted a fraction higher than another. If attuned one can attend the gathering of emotion as weather percolating out at sea . . . for the changes in atmosphere affect the subtle gravities and geographies of the brain.

—S. Dorking, *The Humours of Physics*

<pre>
      sings   us
</pre>
The robin [sang] to make [me] gay
the mournful dove marks our decay
the chafinch busies through her day
the magpies heart in disarray

—Lady Jane Kempsey, *Pieces for Lydia*

The medium of Prophecy is rightfully words. Meanings that unfold in time . . . [a] cluster of signification out of which we must read our meaning. Either the cluster remains meaningless to us . . . or we accept our prophecy . . . as the words are our prediction. Let us not muddy such waters with fantasies of embracing that which has yet to happen . . . prophecy names the next chapter, the roots of which might naturally enough be seen in our current, temporary fixations . . . We ask of Prophecy a resolution which is only this; an opportunity to read.

—William Swan, *The Apocrypha of Being*

some do with dogs upon the screen
to hide our human loneliness
some home with animals for (their) defence
when no-one is come home

Do triangles make inroads on the stars

I had to let myself beyond myself

When your words pour over me or your words become my only
constantly I am appalled by marrow called as others would. Ambivalence
at any moment lover love I could not hold you any other way but throw
you off as close. My self the evening says my dubious self the morning
says and keenly I recall a time where I at least least liked this self—at
least I hold it hollow nut shell small above its puddle rattled free—but
like it less and less for all it would for me. The quiet rueful King in
ecstasy degenerate heir—disaffected organcy outraged rag displaying.
What can I say alone what can I I alone can say.

The eye not seeing at this distance

for in reality, as we know, everything is always quite different.

the vile chimera—distinct and vicious

In the still summer morning children have been taken
Parents in the theatre of mourning
Such as this

In the quiet space of light where Children lay hidden
Parents asking questions
for themselves

Screaming cottage still beside the place
this swallow cuts and cuts
like hopeless night is gone a bit

I am a dilettante curtain lifter.

> Shelley—translation of Goethe's *Faust,* Part One (A. Halsey)

---

a walk the day after an event through a familiar city (not of one's birth)
where orientation depends upon fixing a relation to two or three major
thoroughfares, that despite years visiting such a place are mistaken one
for the other, or when one assumes that a slight bend in a main arterial
road is insignificant, that the road runs true east to west, and again and
again one is surprised when one recognizes one has walked miles out
of one's way.

Edinburgh, Liverpool, London and Sheffield

Today the coach rather than the train, as describing fine curves and
arcs through narrow car lined streets—the original aim of the driver
adjusted and shuddered by the unaccountable and inevitable conflict
with the designs of other drivers. Not to affect one, as a passenger
without responsibilities, small shop fronts and poor shop fronts
through Leeds and Manchester.

I worry about the construction of canals—not sufficiently to research
their building. How a volume of water can be circumvented, how a
sturdy stone bridge can be fixed to banks of grass and earth, and lower
the foundations in the motion of a canal bottom. The most sturdy
looking of pavements, of buildings, when lifted open reveals a porous
pipe and wired filled crevice—a giant honeycomb network
undermining the whole of the city. what we are all rested on ever
shifting and shifting platform. A flotilla.

The structure of questions assumes the possibility of an answer.

An observation without desire to build a universe upon.

I cannot descend to the base
The path-way nettled or conditions ill-advised
with insufficient resources (supplies)
I cannot climb nor descend to the base

a glass to see his (own) filthiness (filthy face)
the tenderest office of a friend
cannot delight decipher find or make
how well when all is done

. . . poetry arizes from difference . . .
—Swan, The Non-Dramatic Works

. . . to make a new-sense of oneself . . .
—ibid.

"Now, for the poet, he nothing affirms, and therefore never lieth."
—Sidney, An Apology

Now ye shall have three ladies walk to gather flowers and then we must
believe the stage to be a garden . . .
—Sir P Sidney, Apology for Poetry

yes yes I was on the outside of the stage this bitter day till I was
severely chilled.

I am leading a posthumous existence
—Keats. Keats House Aug 10, 2000

FOR CHARLIE DRUCE'S MISSING TREE

(Sotto Voce)
Yes Yes I think I can hear you
No not a thing   still
Just Early—while (it was) fresh
mostly outside

Yes yes I'm glad. No (inaudible)
Sorry. Glad

GREETINGS   POST CARD   ADDRESS

FUGUE

It opens well
    if There you love
    trust then to (their) own   trust them to die/(to) let them die
(their) death which they prepare   which is their own
    longer than you have

    Those long in years
    those older than yourselves   (those) younger (than yourself)
    let them as you must   to/be themselves
    leave them so   much as you

    These eyes in flesh
    translating (light) to light   Moving through London
            (Moving) by Tourist Coach (Moving)

In transit then positioned plants
in temporary containers (pots/positions on the porch)
what damages determines blight
Re visiting & visiting the Poets house
(one of the Poet's houses)

What (you let/will) happen   last will
Only Seven years ago   to go
When we first met   before we met
tell (me/you) the truth   tell me something (else/new)

Do not enlist the Thames to glide
nor come into the world after the fair
against the serpent melancholy struggling
in the arms of two or three towards
St. Clement thence to chichester
That understanding may make its appearance and depart

The author suffer to correct his doubt

Out to vast indifference
a complicated sky
where (Constable) Sunday
happens needlessly & necessarily

That's where you had your life
That's where you're having yours
Your countryside Your Cottage [Flat or City] digs
Mines over there—Mines underneath

It is gulls now (in Cheltenham) as the rains come on
(Swallows were on the line) blown over from the estuary
As if you give a shit

"when a man is capable of being in uncertainties, mysteries, doubts,
without any irritable reaching after fact."
                    —Keats, *New York Times Book Review*. Sept. 3rd, 2000

"I'd completely had it with melody. I just wanted rhythm. All
melodies to me were pure embarrassment."
                    —Thom Yorke, *Daily Telegraph*. August 31st, 2000

"by the hand, Silent"

                    —Shakespeare, *NYT* Arts & Leisure.

My bed shall be under the green wood tree
A tuft of bracken under me
from my life I daily flee
for fear of meeting the greenwood tree.

it fell against the next night
the fox was through our bin
the wood pigeon was early up
A cooing

twelve struck through after—have
how struck through before hay
heaven and leaving alternate
as litill and lytyll prety boy

A world of preparation not enough
(to make a speech as this)
And if am eloquent will hate my eloquence
as expert to emotions which one never is

TOWNS

LONDON

Squared miles upon
closed open shutter
dusk yellow-mirror lantern
street legs street taxi drain

plane trees forgiven lawn
brick stone and alabaster gown
society en guilds
My Steeple half a hall on fields

❖

To burst out. I am drowning tonight—I cannot be seen and you cannot hear

The social talk of a celebrity recorded for publication

❖

Your age (my love) I am old when age applies
commands when youth experience her eye
brown as a berry white as
no part of you is yet astray—I am in part
escaped into some out-of-reach
forgotten and must count each part which
hot is now most cold and touch which was
my all is now my absent host
eyes will adjust to gloom ears to din
add sweet to salt "like moths by light attracted and repelled"
a wood grew into a green wood so
your arm and leg the next neck fell

LONDON

Grand Barge upon the Thames
When here in winter held
by tidal tables plot our selves
the Bridge and Dove compelled

the same grey graves
glass cover us in newspaper
Naval disaster foreign plight
hence refugee in arms

most distant by sea
or air—silver cellar
salt cured manny (marley) bone
By cryst your crypt measure your dome

Good Evening—I am not myself this evening, that is, what I say I am told to say—this goes for the actor and the author. As for yourself— you will flatter, wander away, but be assured, your impulse may be flight from the text, but gravity requires you read. The Earth is not firm, or is. You are a temperature.

We are arms about and about each other—for you more lambent, as I beg and gravitate. You commit, cajole. You feature me. Nothing empty in this sequent.

Body sacculated—retulant and sallow. For this instant we provide a tadpole body, gills wearing out—lungs.

I wander this amnesiac
I cannot as I have Love you
to make our basement
attic out of afternoon

yet can ear witness
ever returned to him the name
Man or Sin or whore of Babylon
who never could divide myself from any man

I must confess my greener studies
pollute with the old and obsolete
where constant change a nation of exility
a cancelled present restoration meet

my heads disposed to schism
and complexity propense to innovate
nor ever confined unto order
or economy of one incarnate

mince myself to atoms
retaining something of the author yet
his name or Cenotaph
I believe he was dead

❖

I am now content to understand a mystery without a rigid definition
                    —Sir Thomas Browne, *Religio Medici*

The increase and the decrease of the Nile
The world is still as though it had not been
the grit is in its place—the leaf correct
conversion of the needle to the north

many articles of me—my lover
who is best as her own story
my past protection documentary
eclipse—expect a reunion forever

will you in your gleeful robe
invite at last a vision incomplete
ly sated like a dog each meal
forgotten and enjoyed and

livd here for thirty years
his daughters were all
no one saw him there
A newspaper

Vision at the table, table cloth
dark cupboard opened slightly
slightly imperceptibly ajar
to nothing just before it in the sun

these are our best knives (from Sheffield, bone handles)
We amass some glasses such as these
to entertain ourselves our friends
Have another please

You should see my shoes (his shoes)
Collected over years, shoe trees
these shirts were made for me
I bought these

Mercury downward into surface
superficial things say
we are coming from our sacrifice
(Three words removed from the Dictionary)

fa(c)ulty (T)heat(re)
War(mth) (hur)ting(e) (thr)eat

Satisfied with some Etruscan Pie

(T)rust(ing) can/(tin)
ma(i)n(ly) (ly)in(g)
(H)ope(ratio)n (T)rut(h)
Came(l)
Ca(r)me(l)it(e) h(e)ave(n)/(not)
author(ship) b(r)east
le(av)es wor(l)ds (c)old

Dish(eve)led Man(ner)/or

Will somebody please shut up

I am, however, young and writing at random, straining after particles
of light in the midst of a great darkness, without knowing the
bearing of any one assertion, of any one opinion—yet, in this may I
not be free from sin?

—Keats

with one eye shut
my face has fallen off
stop at Winchester
for a fish supper

I rise from the table hungry
I am these days always hungry

with pigtails like my preety little gymnast
a vision straddle-beam my an eye-mast
if bitch afford you no dynastic wish
Her ursinity (Young, soccer-squat—furred shins)

When I am richest matter they follow me by moments

—Archangel Roberts

ON THE TRINITY
Footnote to a commentary of Donne's Anniversaries

Consciousness has the good of knowing itself. When consciousness and object are one—there is no more death. Death is already metaphoric in the realm of consciousness, when we contemplate death without consciousness ending.

Knowledge then is self-knowledge. Self-Knowledge or self-consciousness is not simply a sub set of knowledge. It is knowledge to accept a direct relation between what we know and what is knowable. This is then the merging of subject and object. It is tantamount to death—or the acceptance of the consciousness of the self as other. It is the undeath/death in immanence. We are our knowledge of the world. Thus the realm of consciousness intercedes between that which would be self and that which would be world. A unity in trinity.

—Ambrose Greene, Speculum

What now—secondary—the reason
(s) we try to write for (seasons) honestly
I can hardly imagine myself anymore
There is this quick function from recordings

Comeback to me—here I am again
let me tell you something of this creature
Try(all) w(h)is(p)er
Why I try to kiss those women

END OF PLAY

An Opera tentatively entitled "The Philosopher's Head." Projected onto the head of a single body. The individual described by an influence of voices.

Reader: (Object book such as this, table such as this, Reader such as this)
Book: (in lieu of)

Scene Opens—Light. Representing Future / Past Hope / Reflection Happiness / Nostalgia

Author's Notes [the scene is poignant—to our reader this represents the vital. The scene is to be absent of all mimicry—objects, slippery at the best of times to be kept to a minimum]

Costume—[the element of Costume as telling as the script—clothes of the actor in relation to those of the audience, and of their expectations. A cloak for example offering a dramatic contrast. A black suit—the sort an audience may imagine themselves capable of wearing though they seldom wearing in reality—gestures with the hands, cut of the hair, posture].

Recipe for Galantine
What people may have eaten besides this: poached egg on toast

Period of Performance. Matinee / Eve. Season. Consideration of those other plays popular this season. Revival of Favourite Musical, Renowned performance of a Shakespeare tragedy, Festival of Experimentation.

Door (again representing). Transom of Cobalt (see Novalis). Curtain (see Nietzsche)

Priamel: (vase of piss-a-beds) He went hence but now
                              And certainly in strange unquietness

Curtain lifts to vacated scene. Light as mentioned
Before the audience a book:
(Unspoken aside)   were the black noteless page a mirror to the
truest self
          were one word upon the page an opening—admittance of (default)
          the audience might then for a small while contemplate the book
          Acknowledge their own part—thus far their noises as they wait

The path before us is all puddle (mirror) Author's veneer. Enter Cast:
Priamel cont.
          Strike out that Gulf! What is this now between us
          I am not safely housed away from this
          My life is by another so in other words
          How can I rest when where I am is else

          Cause cause and defection
          a voice in me is calling all I am
          prove laughter a collapse, prove wailing so
          manage a report to show it some

          plucked here these dandelions will not last the hour
          but where they landed there they start out from
          as though a cistern were a fountain
          clearly this glass is looking to be seen

          empty. Let nothing
          hold this nothing and we are. Let nothing
          written on this book read yet determine
          where we meet upon this set

Contradiction is one of the devices not in itself a sufficiency. The mark of the lyric is an impulse matched by its opposition—though not simply a balance. Paradox is a swinging of energies. Thus ends the notebook marked NOTA

poetry can inhabit a profitable ambiguity. It carries the burden of its writing. To make something away from the self (the detritus of the religious feeling). To experience is in some degree to suffer. To experience a sensation in the order of pain.

Our relation to the eternal in Ennius:
> "Let no one grace my grave with tears! For why?
> I live upon men's lips eternally . . ."

Poetry: The exaggerated indulgences of a mind bored by its own body's inactivity. No longer the mind busy with protection—no longer the mind bothered at the body's well being. Poetry is exactly the manifestation of a mandarin state. The human reminded of its animal ancestry—the body. The mind occupying its day. Sufficient to say perhaps I am my own worst enemy. We are our own worst enemy. What are we to do with doing?

—William Swan, *The Apocrypha of Being*

Something threw a bird into my line of vision.
poverty and suffering ennoble only when they are voluntary

people are multiplying their wants

Thank God you didn(o)t make it home with me
My urge must have intolerate your breath
hair as it was held up and out not earnestly
Youth's flagrant mole youth's blank embroidery

Put a flower on this
that I might be as they

sight of the Egyptian punt in green water
from below

Egyptian punt seen from below
pump out the reservoir reveals
the scattered bodies were not there before

here and there in the ocean waste, a swimmer's seen
violin-fault errs to news
Can make no head against being material
The body is her stay (he dips a little musical)
brain, spleen, myrach, hypochondries
too hot too cold the brain (a miseryrhyme for the moon)
bad diet bad air retention of abundant seed
some sleep some laugh in lavender or rosemary
the interrupt these that lean appall confound me
another dares no bridge come near a pond intent to hurt him
rock, steephill, for fear he will precipitate himself
something unfit to be said pensive without cause
an agony for toys a barking dog this feral plague
molested if they speak small compliment complaint
they do I do and by-and-by repent
upon a spoken word a thousand dangers and discouragement

some broken property torments
content without estates
                              and yet desirous to a state
hare sitting in her form attempts
                              contriving potentates

❖

It is some disaster then
these night after night
of setting down the self
a glass two eyes roll down

The water particle
The bend in light
at any pace
self-turn over and inside a face

Servetus had rejected the doctrine of predestination on the grounds that it denied human freedom—see Bainton, page 138. Was this then an assertion of freedom, to reject predestination—or was Servetus's action predictable, or, not even that, a simple manifestation of a complex of influences.

—S. Dorking, *Nota Nusquam*

. . . we may say spiritual illumination is "common to all men" but is that life of Henry More bright like that of Thomas Traherne or Dame Julian . . .

The messages stand by their own strength

we are not capable of change individually . . . but only via the energy of a dynamic relation . . . dry needs wet to moisten . . . man is alive as clay . . . dead as dust.

God is the essence of all created things 'all things are a part and portion of God . . . God fills all things, even hell.'

—Servetus

why should the heart be held accountable . . . no more than the meat of the hand . . . but that it ache at times . . . that it pains.

M: Master it, call yourself together here

VOICE: Having heard her speak
EYE: Aye, I cannot look—her face
         [Coward of your life]
VOICE: she presses on you
EYE: comes close to this [some manner of gesture]
M: one muscle weakness
VOICE: But what is that
         [Flight of Free Radicals]
EYE: look at me, obsequious
M: demented from purpose
VOICE: humorous decline
M: mirror my invention
EYE: world
VOICE: my vocation's evocation

THE SELF-CRUEL

cast that glass away
Nor in its crystal face its own survey
burns from this mirror rise
by the reflected beams of its own eyes

FAULTES ESCAPED IN THE WEEDES

FOL.	LINE	FAULTES	CORRECTIONS
211	17	like I hope	I like hope
216	28	merrye	married
218	7	called	calling
220	14	had	and
222	30	in	of
223	7	And	so
224	7	Cape	Cappe
ibid.	8	Crowe	Crowne
235	19	possessed	professed
242	11	and	an
249	13	builded	blinded
275	2	swell	aswell
278	6	that I	I that
284	8	But	this
285	14	this	those

Enfeebled

If first my feeble head, have so much matter left
hang
                                    teeth unkempt this trebling tongue
wan raging force may stand patterns for a ghost
These shoulders they sustain bruised yoke
A forge plays the smith
knees bellows our hungry corps say
what was he that you have worn
to nought. today

---

starred and daggered footnotes are his own
rais'd orgies thrown
when locks arouse the reigning shine
and oiled walls delight our prisoner
into whose pocket shall I find
the absence of obedience divine

WHEN I CLOSE MY EYES

The light is silent. A considerable weight is lifted put upon. In this
dark the weight of your blood—blood coloured. out to the regions of
touch.

There is no story of this moment. Past wars. The animal that never
was. Great shoulders of Yew cannot sustain a leaden sky. The weight
is considerable. Inconceivable. In Autumn of November when it is
still blue. When a low light comes from the leaves of an opposite
sycamore. Or when an evening light passes through the last leaves of
a sycamore. Or when a car passes. Of any description really. And a
squirrel the same as itself tugged by anxiety. Nowhere to support
such weight. The gold establishes the blue. Florentine. Not like them.
not in character.

The noise of our body can be felt. A notable phrase passes. Not a
frieze. Though one appreciates that sentiment. What reprehensible
activity can bring me to myself. This ancient craft of avoidance. My
abuse. The bulk of self arbitrarily exaggerated. Close like this I can
tell the gravity of close walls—or Great Yews. For years I had kept
one eye open. And conversely. The sloth not less terrified than the
mouse. As though a glove were all of subtle glass. A sheath. It is
capillaries. somewhat filled with silver. shivers blood. The surface of a
lake will calm and quickly as I pass. What I see, most terrified, in my
assailants eye. many live in sorrow. That I cannot kill love. At night all
his thoughts are afflictions. Their terror is animal. Their response.

If I can drag this dead weight to a thought. Though feeding a hunger.
Not that. Why is this other people's city not my own. Brief
invocation. lightless reflection. this air cold. enervating. You would
settle for your body's temperature. A plant closes. words in
themselves are true? where else this bewildered head. A plain.

perhaps invisible. warm water can be made to ice. continually for myself. the heralded shout I am wrong. Am I wrong. The despised despise me also. The wise disagree. The worldly can find me no world. what matter. Light the colour of my eyes. blood blue. blind into the world. great children. stings abounding. living pain. My blood bellows in the dark. Its own ocean. wings in unison. A flock of night starlings. this cold season beaks against the granite faced dictator.

The luxury of not attaining. Always attainable. delicious in the bath the not quite body of my dreams. Calamitous din many streets away. one with a stick rains blows. the dogs in this neighbourhood abarking. awareness is approval. some desire. miles over the city. Signature smoke-stacks. cog-teeth factories. slick canal. dogged river. once named in a poem for its beauty. such. our hero. sufficiently attired. not lucky. through to his desires quickly in this dream. digs. sufficiently attired. grotesque burden. sag bedded volume. limbs akimbo in a last wrack yawn. beggarly. "Finish my teeth then I will come and help". a nervous foray where he should not be. the door ajar. the children with their television companions. this one may be asleep. but honestly she does not seem to mind. this whole town. white thigh. brown. enveloped. a dog publicly. a boy in the next room. a phonecall under the bath water. canal. a corpse bourne up by magistrates. Most of this is admissible. but the boy yearning through his stagnation. strike the magistrates. that came in from the outside later. a postcard of a film.

cock eating the chicken. the black of that eye I have it held somewhere. this imagery. all dressed for public approval/ disapproval/disavowal. I hardly care. This most important of moments. At one time sharp objects or the unfair malice of opponents. Now it is the whole shit bellied carnival. a Burlesque in drag. a face in piccolo. rambunctious fellows in their high drawn knickers titupping. prancing. regular as a bundle. sad as a puppy. flat as a fucked ham sandwich. in my giddy stew again. bear with me. burdensome this. significant arenas might be: The Diary. The City Walls. The Portico. The Pier. Stations a whole set.

My body has been listening to this all the while. exhausted in its libidinopus ruination. spitting off the bridge at our faces in the sky below. swans eating. The brown-schlonged corpse's last indignity. then the next. Acknowledged subjects of the conversation necessarily disbursed. The attention of the body's angle. References to laws. law breaking. the description of self as bill of sale. barker announcements of aggression or simple-minded honesty as ploys for self advancement the desire to achieve status. to achieve satiety. to achieve a room of lovers numerous positions available. negotiate terms. bicker. fly off.

The end of the dream is perhaps its degeneration into a discernible metaphor. its use outweighs its value. for I am closed eyed but not dreaming. as this must show. sober insufficient being. In the dark limits come out of their corner to heckle the senses. Why should one despise one's tools. my second face wriggling uncomfortably. A shadow spokesperson. This job could this way be done better.

The simple task of lying. eyes close the tell you the truth. take stock. seasoning. reminiscent of earlier times which were. several times. most of the past takes place. in the course of a week. until a jolt and I have a nice new past. how long have you been telling yourself. in my dark room cabinet. placed in the midst. at the teetering brink. the senseless rising and falling. floored by the lid off the whole kit.

imagine yourself hungry. but longer. two legs pushed to release. chin back where it wants under the throat eyes roll to the back to the top and nose bone. all things that come to the ground. All this to fuck a roomfull. not specific. lust. because it does not matter. I am so bored by your babies. by your babying babies. yap yapping dogs. the gulls sound terrified at the catch. haul it in and look over it in awe. mother of all oceans. the net's burden. indispensible.

Ah me. what sweet thoughts. a happy time in wretchedness. picking over. we had been after. can you find a moment alone. that would be as much. the rain makes them howl like dogs. because they are dogs. they often turn themselves. in my state I had become a great worm. The world around me insisted. fists into my yetching throat. ribbed throat. hard when I thought it would be soft. Any body is better than none. I can't imagine. I languish in the rain. but out of it. settle in any room with any fellow. the crime befits the punishment. we are trying to listen to each other. your body drops as though another has let it go. Plutus, the god of riches and Pluto, the god of the lower regions are indistinguishable. that dismal bank. what would you throw away. If you were able. the prescient fire.

You write to me and I am afire. defending myself with books. uninhibited without a cause. a body. the ambitions of a god. why on earth would anybody make anybody in their image. Jesus! Pegasus! can you help it. enough seepage of water and you have a river. but I could not imagine it. we always come to the foot of a tower.

my ambitions to start anew. to leap full off with you into our own. a cascade. a tumultitude of. no body is to blame. but this pad floating in front of an imaginary audience. I close my eyes. a lie. what it wants is my death. a stop to this very hope. to be loved. to sex beyond my performance. machismo doesn't manage a full sentence. we all read a little. you realize do you realize. when I write. even in medias res. embarassed alive. to build is ambition. to love is not to build. but to. why pretend.

the telephone. occasional parties of having managed intercourse. my authority. so seldom my own authority. no wonder one's distance from earth. or perhaps this too is prejudice. I am not afterall ploughing a field. which in itself would not be.

CANTO I

But not the eyes opening

Painting is the manipulation of light. nobody remembers to manipulate as much as nature. when we leave home we do not expect you to break in. this can never happen with a poem.

Areas of longing. The telephone. where it is. not the image of the other. neither of oneself. not the object itself. 3 feet away from oneself. or that voice in a wartime cabinet. A shelter. Brought to you by. for example somebody else on the phone whilst you are in the room. in the room is not sufficient. maybe thirty pages. the news. which comes to us courtesy. something in that other room. breaks open the realm of the voice. places one in a field against a wall. observing. a gesture. not against a wall. we have a white cat come to visit which allows us to feel privileged. when one is on the phone. somehow absent.

a book will. when I look away. and then when I look back to the spot I left. my body remembers. I had not realized. I had written one to be read. mostly. by myself. and then I got confused. but with another book it is just mine. a fruit picked and put down. I move some things around in the kitchen where they mostly stay until we leave. Girlhood. wearing this. thin. I am precious scared of this. glass-egg. It is my own fault not to drop this. inherited. when she opens her legs. to herself. The three-legged stool. dressing table. no need to mention. curls inside an envelope. It's not for me to say. Brer rabbit. The mischievous hedgerow owl. decoy. highly
polished. briars. pimples. soap.

Transport. stations. similar even to the greengrocers. an attempt at a descriptive gesture self-conscious adoption (misappropriation) of mores. acknowledgement of oneself as indistinct. not pleasurable perhaps. or weddings. they don't trust me. Or. they trust me. That is. one reflects a certain insecurity. please move along. what you chose to wear.

can it just be this moment. then the next. I have some interest in this matter. keep telling myself. such as sex. interest in achievement. but then it continues. bit through to my teeth. are you somebody with a particular haircut. so people recognize me. this indicates a desire. How do you stand it. I can hardly stand it. This even sounds like something.

light recalls the shadow to its body. the shadow dominates in both realms. hence we are hopeful towards light. jealous of light. our skin most sensitive to its weight. incipient sepulchre. noumenon. hisself enclitic. days camera.

CANTO II

The days complete. another. marshalling complexity. the fleet is in cries above the harbour. light joggles on the ink. what we have been waiting for. looking forward to. is another way. a climax to it all. jostling complexities of Aneurin, Alcuin, Auden. Over the night water. farmer long abed. shepherd huddled. salesperson extended over complexities of cables. the driver prone. experts in their position. where the mother of our future. I have any.

We don't leave this winter. make yourself an audience. you all died and it meant nothing.

I made it to my throat. to say something about. people. making it. happen. hooting. this is how I woke up.

CANTO III

If you have forgotten. I still have them closed. not much to it. If I am making a parcel to take with me. Sir J. Suckling perhaps or perhaps some minor Caroline poet. I like that minor. institutionalize obscurity. its in the book. look me up. some time. I have meant very little for a good while. a long time. Campion and Townshend have built almost nothing to perfection. thank heavens. nobody really minds. thank heavens. there are still one or two shirts. I am saving. for what. I am annoyed about that tear. what it shows. what it reveals. to me is that I have no idea about any of it really. through no fault of my own. I enjoy the minor poets. this Sunday .whilst I am waiting to go out. I shall just wear this.

I happen to have forgotten. That's all about me.

CANTO IV

Relative. Ambrose Smith. the celebrants tinnitus. you cannot from
one point to another by movement. you are already over there. ever-
recurring state of individual consciousness. suffering and sighing all
sighs and all human ambitions.

my young sitter. sister. dressed after washing. combing her black
down. it is okay. fine. my heart is hot in its cavity. timid I am as
anything. without invitation. my planet slips in front of me. like. a
giant planet. I have yet to write. as promised. of my relative.

Areas of achievement
food. which can be easily. cheese such as history. in my hunger where
my skin fits. size regular. made to extend to this.

If I cannot believe it is decoration. the antipodes resemble. nature as a
tribute. the dog will not envy us inventions. their reeking city. cock
spindle drools a tendon.

CANTO NEXT

The time chosen is early morning. The landscape is an eastward view
of the country, as it may be supposed to have appeared in its time,
interspersed with cottages and villages; some buildings and spires
indicate the situation of the Great City. A proper advantage is taken
of this circumstance to describe the subject of the Picture. The
Characters are the characters which compose all ages and nations, for
we see the same characters repeated in animals, vegetables, minerals
as in humankind. Nothing new occurs in identical existence. Every
age is a pilgrimage. The ploughman is Hercules in his supreme. The
engine replaces nothing. such exists in all times and places for our
trial. To astonish every neighbourhood with brutal strength. the new
era is of no incomprehensible nature. a parent. collapses.
In this new imagined light. There are always Grand Houses. The face
of which. wallways. in this new imagined light. the walls aureate
white. a hand cast thin blue. vein wrist. formidable shutters.

ownership is elsewhere. which does not stop. collapses.

his or her bicycle. fetishized. saddle of course. lent one on one. hired
or borrowed. owned. the occasion. A 45th birthday to which nobody
is invited. invitations to which. shutters. vein blue. bottle of greasy
amber. pour.

not even his daughter. blue. or the trappings. blue. we never get. a
view over the table.

CANTO NEXT

Sphery. Jealous of myself my loves the one who this deserves. Halt.
half-headed. Jaw blubbed down in drool. banged in in weather.
fencing sticky to itself. savage in the dales. the poorest animal. Are
you forgetting.

Vegetation which I call out to. but not as though I knew. the ocean
more like vegetable. the mountains in this part more like. ourselves
more or less like vegetable. I brush past an animal which cant be me.
its static rush. I am continually surprised. in hiding. this vegetable
part. fattened as I am on Human blood. lust in a bursting part. my
splintered knees. hiding my books burying my desires in increments
burying my books and hands and books. bargaining myself.

blood bubble at my lips. nothing spectacular. mucous at the face. in
the soil. nothing to remark upon. satisfactication. cities. ride up the
side. of great empty.

Quake. we hope. destroy. we hope. property. we are appalled at it.
look what is left. oh my god. we said. oh my fucking hur. then
broken off. one thing that is called china. I am still unsure. one thing
that is rain. or ceiling. these. I am still unsure. or. quiet. peaceably
long. in my dress. lain down now in my pissy ruddy stock.

FENCEbooks

FENCE was launched in the spring of 1998. A biannual journal of poetry, fiction, art and criticism, *Fence* has a mission to publish challenging writing distinguished by idiosyncrasy and intelligence rather than by allegiance with camps, schools, or cliques. *Fence* has published works by some of the most esteemed contemporary writers as well as excellent writing by the completely unknown. It is part of our mission to support young writers who might otherwise have difficulty being recognized because their work doesn't answer to either the mainstream or to recognizable modes of experimentation.

FENCEbooks is an extension of that mission: With our books we provide expanded exposure to poets and writers whose work is excellent, challenging, and truly original. **The Alberta Prize** is an annual series administered by Fence Books in collaboration with the Alberta duPont Bonsal Foundation. The Alberta Prize offers publication of a first or second book of poems by a woman, as well as a five thousand dollar cash prize.

Our second prize series is the **Fence Modern Poets Series**. This contest is open to poets of either gender and at any stage in their career, and offers a one thousand dollar cash prize in addition to book publication.

For more information about either prize, visit our website at **www.fencebooks.com**, or send an SASE to: Fence Books/[Name of Prize], 303 East Eighth Street, Buzzer B1, New York, New York, 10003.

For more about *Fence,* visit **www.fencemag.com**.

FENCEbooks

Nota
Martin Corless-Smith

Apprehend
Elizabeth Robinson
2003 FENCE MODERN POETS SERIES

Father of Noise
Anthony McCann

The Real Moon of Poetry and Other Poems
Tina Brown Celona
2002 ALBERTA PRIZE

The Red Bird
Joyelle McSweeney
2002 FENCE MODERN POETS SERIES

Can You Relax in My House
Michael Earl Craig

Zirconia
Chelsey Minnis
2001 ALBERTA PRIZE

Miss America
Catherine Wagner